MW01258014

She
is
Visible

Dr. Andrea Williams

Dr. Andrea Williams

She
is
Visible

Dr. Andrea Williams, Th.D, D.Min

Andrea
Williams
Ministries

She is Visible

Dedication

There are people God sends into your life at just the right time—for the right reason.

To Bishop James E. Blue, Jr.

You were one of those divine appointments. A man who not only spoke strength into my life but lived out your belief in me every step of the way. You didn't just open doors—you *stood in the doorway* to make sure it stayed open for me. Your love, wisdom, and unwavering support gave me energy when I had none, and hope when I needed it most. Though I miss you deeply in the natural realm, your voice still echoes in my spirit. Your encouragement lives on—in this book and in my becoming.

To my brothers—Marlon, Sherman, and Dewayne

Thank you for always holding up my arms. For seeing me. For reminding me of who I am even when I doubted myself. You've loved me through every phase of my process, and your quiet strength has carried me more times than you know. You've never let me forget that I was born to be visible—and I honor you for that.

To my sons—Norman and Quinn,

Watching you become fathers has been one of the greatest joys of my life. You're raising daughters now—brilliant, beautiful, and full of purpose. This is my heart to you: Make sure they know how visible they are. Cover them in love and truth. Cheer for them loudly. Never let their light be dimmed by the world around them. Teach them that their voices matter, their gifts are needed, and their presence shifts atmospheres. You are their first mirror, reflect back to them the greatness God has placed within.

And Calvin, who is raising sons of destiny, teaching them to cheer for their sisters and for themselves…

To all of you—thank you.
For your love.
For your belief in me.
For helping me stay visible.
This book is for you.

ENDORSEMENTS

She Is Visible:
A Prophetic Journey from Silence to Sacred Voice
By Dr. Andrea Williams

Dr. Patricia Gould-Champ: Virginia Union University, Assistant Professor of Practical Theology:
It has been said that the greatest sin women are challenged with is the "sin of hiding". This book helps to confront this challenge by giving women the inspiration, wisdom, and tools needed to move from hiding to being fully visible, and from silence to being comfortable with hearing their own voices. *She is Visible* weaves through the journey from silence to sacred voice with the care that only a seasoned Womanist Pastor such as Dr. Andrea Williams can offer. I recommend this offering to both lay and clergy women who seek to be made whole and to be empowered to walk in their full authenticity. This is a much needed resource for both the academy and the church. It is my hope that it will not only be read but received into the hearts of all women who sincerely desire to move from silence to their God-ordained sacred voice.

From the Desk of Pastor Debra Jordan
- Zoe Ministries | New York, NY | May 12, 2025
Dr. Andrea,
It is with great honor and deep spiritual alignment that I extend my wholehearted endorsement for She Is Visible: A Prophetic Journey from Silence to Sacred Voice by Dr. Andrea Williams. This work is more than a literary offering; it is a clarion call to the daughters of destiny who have been silenced for far too long. Dr. Williams masterfully pens a sacred path that awakens the hidden, heals the wounded, and reclaims the fullness of womanhood with prophetic clarity. Every chapter reads like a

mirror and a mantle, reminding women that our voice is not only valid, but it is vital.

I encourage every reader, leader, and seeker of divine truth to engage this book as a sacred tool for restoration and bold transformation.

With prophetic blessing,

Pastor Debra A. JordanZoe Ministries

Dr. Nyakya T. Brown - Psychotherapist, Transformative Coach; Mayor of South Floral Park, NY

"She Is Visible: A Prophetic Journey from Silence to Sacred Voice" is a powerful manifesto for women who have lived unseen and unheard, now called to reclaim their rightful place with grace and authority. Dr. Andrea Williams masterfully guides readers from silence to sacred revelation, affirming that every woman's voice is both necessary and revolutionary. With prolific eloquence and fierce determination, this work invites us to confront the shadows that silence creates, empowering us to rise boldly into visibility. It is more than just a book—it is a declaration, a summons, an anthem of dignity, resilience, and freedom. [This is] essential reading for every woman ready to speak truth, stand firm, and transform silence into triumphant song.

Apostle Robyn Williams, M.Ed., M.S.Ed

If there were a cautionary note for She is Visible: A Prophetic Journey from Silence to Sacred Voice, it would be: "Prepare for Frequent Stops."

Dr. Williams maps out a prophetic path that becomes deeply personal, crafted with phrases that serve not just as punctuation but as FULL STOP moments. The narrative invites sacred pauses where the Spirit does transformative work.

This book leads readers out of unhealthy silence and into healing. With prophetic precision and compassion, Dr. Williams exposes wounds, uproots limiting beliefs, and plants truths that restore voice and purpose.

Wherever you are on your journey, She is Visible offers a moment of clarity - whether you need a check-up or deep healing. It is revelatory, restorative, and essential.

Dr. Williams, your work is a feast of healing. As an apostle, prophet, and scholar, you've set a table for sacred voices to rise. To that we say, "Yes, chef!" Brava.

Minister Kim Cochran - Entrepreneur, REALTOR®, Business Owner, Women's Empowerment Leader:
There are books you read—and then there are books that read you.
She Is Visible doesn't just speak to you—it speaks for you.
If you've ever known what it feels like to vanish beneath responsibility, resilience, or religious expectation, these pages will feel like breath. Like memory. Like fire returning to the altar of your becoming.

Dr. Andrea Williams has not merely written a book—she has released a movement in manuscript form. Her words carry the weight of revelation and the tenderness of a midwife, guiding women through their most sacred rebirths. Her voice is unapologetically honest, poetically rich, and prophetically sound. Each chapter uncovers a new layer of becoming, reminding us that our power was never lost—only buried beneath silence, shame, or survival.

She Is Visible is for every woman who has ever felt muted, minimized, or misunderstood. Through these pages, Dr. Andrea becomes both scribe and guide, showing us that visibility is not vanity—it is victory.

I didn't just read this book.
I remembered myself in it.

Jesaira L. Glover-Dulin - Ph.D. Candidate

She Is Visible is an answer to the secret cry echoing in the spirits of women across generations. For too long, society has demanded that we shrink, silence ourselves, and contort our identities to fit narratives that were never ours to begin with. But no more.

In this bold and necessary work, Dr. Andrea doesn't just write, she **declares**. Her prophetic voice rises as a trumpet call, catapulting women into unapologetic **ACCEPTANCE** of their God-ordained identity. This book is a clarion call to the daughters of the Divine: **the hour of the woman is now**, and the era of seeking permission is over.

She Is Visible dismantles religious dogma and patriarchal distortion that have long kept women bound, invisible, and out of alignment with their true essence. This book doesn't just inspire it activates. It is about **liberation**, **confirmation**, and **complete transformation**.

Dr. Andrea is on assignment—to partner with women globally as they return home to the truth of who they are: **Divine, powerful, sacred, prophetic**. This is not about performance. This is about embodiment. It's about moving from survival and performance into **embodied POWER, divine AUTHORITY, and soul-led ALIGNMENT.**

To every woman who has ever whispered, "There has to be more…"—this is your answer.

Congratulations, Dr. Andrea, on birthing such a radical and revolutionary offering. *Woman, you are visible—and now the whole world must reckon with your light.*

TABLE OF CONTENTS

Chapter 1: The Shrouded Citadel – The Revealer

The fog came first—
Thick.
Breathless.
Blinding.

It wrapped around her like gauze, clinging to her skin, curling into her lungs.

No sky above.
No earth beneath.
Only the quiet murk of the in-between.

She didn't remember arriving.
She only knew she had always been on her way here.

The Citadel loomed ahead, barely visible through the haze—its walls impossibly high, vanishing into clouds that refused to lift. Its presence hummed—ancient and alert—like it had been waiting for her. Or someone like her.

She moved forward, barefoot.

The ground beneath was stone, worn by centuries of forgotten feet. Along the wall, faint carvings—nearly erased—scratched remnants of once-bold symbols faded by time and silence.

Her feet ached from the journey she couldn't name.
Dust clung to her skin. Her throat held the taste of memory and metal.

Her fingers reached instinctively for a groove in the stone.
A fragment of a name.
The moment her skin met it—something stirred.

A whisper.

"You are not the first, Daughter of Sight."

The voice was not loud.
It didn't need to be.

It moved through her bones, not her ears.

She froze.
Her heart stuttered.

Daughter of Sight.
How did it know?

She closed her eyes.
The fog pressed closer.

And then—she saw.

Not with her eyes.
With the deeper seeing.

Behind her closed lids, the walls shimmered. Thousands of carvings—once invisible—rose into view. Faces of women etched in forgotten lines. Some regal. Some weathered. Some fierce.

Warriors.
Builders.
Midwives.
Scholars.
Prophets.
Queens.
Outcasts.

Their names had been wiped.
Their stories unraveled.
But not erased.

Only hidden.

The Citadel had not been built to protect.
It had been built to contain.

And she was here to break its silence.

A memory flickered—her grandmother's voice reading aloud names
that never made it into the textbooks.
Women from her lineage who led, who healed, who rose—but who
had been footnoted as "helpers," if named at all.

"We have always been more than they recorded," her grandmother
once whispered.

She pressed her hand to the wall.

Light bloomed beneath her palm—slow, pulsing.
It crawled along the stone, tracing the once-lost carvings,
illuminating each woman etched into the ancient walls.

As the light spread, the fog hissed and recoiled.

"Your task is not to climb, but to uncover."

She walked slowly along the wall, fingers outstretched.
One face at a time.
One memory at a time.

They had not been forgotten.
They had only been waiting to be seen.

A gust of air swept through the corridor.
The mist stirred violently, trying to retake the space.

Then—the voices came.

Not whispers.
Declarations.

"I was a queen, but they called me a servant."
"I was a scholar, but they buried my scrolls."
"I was a builder, but they named men the architects."
"I was a leader, but they erased me from the stones."

The weight of their grief dropped her to her knees.

She pressed her hands flat to the ground, trying to steady herself.

Who am I to carry this?

The fog surged again sweet and deceptive.

"You don't need to do this."
"Someone else can speak."
"Forget. It's safer."

But the wall did not relent.

"We carried it first."
"We endured so you could stand here."
"You are not the first.
But you are not alone."

A deeper voice rose beneath the others.
Not a command.
A knowing.

"You see because you are meant to see."

Her chest heaved. Her hands trembled.
But she did not pull away.

She stood.

The mist thinned—terrified of her rising.

The Citadel walls bloomed with light.
Names.
Faces.
Truths.

She walked forward, whispering:

"I see you."

And the carvings responded:

"And we see you."

At the far end of the Citadel, a section of the wall shimmered—then vanished.
Not a door.
A passage revealed by revelation.

She stepped through it.

The mist parted.

The light behind the stone pulsed once—then dimmed, like breath settling after centuries of holding.

But something else had begun.

The ground shifted.
The air stirred.

A new sound rose—
Not a shout.
Not a whisper.

A hum.
Of voices waiting.

And she realized…

Seeing them was only the beginning.

Now—she would have to hear them.

She didn't come to decode ruins.
She came to reveal the women who had waited in silence for
someone to finally say:

I see you. I hear you. I will remember you.

Narrative Reflection

I used to think "seeing" meant observation.
Standing on the outside, interpreting what was in front of me.
But the Citadel taught me something different.
To truly see is to remember.
To witness what was erased.
To let truth rise from the rubble of forgetting.
The fog I feared wasn't hiding danger—it was hiding me.
And now that I've stepped through it, I'm beginning to see myself,
too.
Not as the one who stumbled into history—
But as the one it was waiting for.

Prophetic Reflection – *Daughter, Arise*

Daughter of Sight,
you who have questioned your clarity—
They called your knowing "too much."
They called your insight "intimidating."
But heaven calls it a gift.
You were never meant to live veiled, edited, or erased.
You were made to expose what was hidden,
to awaken what was forgotten,

to see not just with eyes, but with Spirit.
This is not pride. It's prophecy.
Do not retreat from what you see.
You were anointed for this vision.
Step into it.

She Is Now Visible – *The Revealer*

She sees beneath the surface—
the things no one else names,
the silences that shape rooms,
the truths others bury for comfort.
For years, she stayed quiet.
Not because she didn't see—
but because she thought no one would listen.
But now?
She names what others ignore.
She illuminates what's been obscured.
And when she speaks, it's not to draw attention—
It's to draw truth into the light.
Fog lifts when she walks in.
Because her presence says:
"I see what was hidden.
And I won't look away."

The gate behind her closed without sound.
No latch. No click.
Just a breath released into space.

She stood at the threshold of a chamber so vast; it seemed to inhale
and exhale.
Stone arches stretched endlessly upward, vanishing into shadows.
The air was no longer fogged—
But thick with something older.

Memory.

She stepped forward.

The sound of her movement echoed… and then echoed again.
But it wasn't her own footsteps she heard returning.

It was something deeper.

Other steps.
Other breaths.
Other stories.

The Hall didn't respond with silence.

It responded with layers.

Fragmented. Dissonant.
As if voices had once filled this space and then been sealed inside the
walls.

She walked slowly, each step a declaration.
The stone beneath her feet was etched—not by hands, but by
presence.
Script carved by pain, history, and invisible weight.

A pillar bore a phrase:

"She spoke the truth, and they called it instability."

Another:

"She questioned the order, and they named it rebellion."

A third:

"She remembered, and they said she imagined it."

She paused.

Her eyes welled, but not from sadness.
Recognition.
She had heard versions of those sentences spoken to the women who
raised her.

The ones who weren't afraid to name injustice at the dinner table.
The ones who were told to "calm down" when they resisted erasure.
The ones who held history in their bones, even when the books
refused to name them.

The orb hovered in the center of the Hall.
Not a relic.
A witness.

Cracked.
Glowing softly from within.
Suspended by sorrow and time.

She approached.

The air thickened.
Not with danger—
With attention.

The Hall had awakened.

And now, it waited.

She reached out.

The orb pulsed—once, twice—

And then the stories poured in.

Not in sound.

In impact.

They struck her like waves.

"I was told to wait my turn."
"I was asked to smile while bleeding."
"I was praised for staying silent."
"I was safe as long as I was invisible."

She staggered. Fell to her knees.

How do I hold this?

Around her, the Hall shifted.

Stone walls shimmered, revealing alcoves—dozens, hundreds.
Each one dark.
Each one holding the silence of someone who had not been heard.

She stood—legs shaking, breath shallow—and moved toward the first.

Her hand hovered.

A soft vibration—like a humming voice waiting to sing again.

She whispered:

"You were not erased. You were silenced.
But I am here now.
I hear you."

The alcove lit.

From the shadows stepped a woman.
Shimmering. Steady.
She nodded once—then dissolved into light.

At the next alcove:

"They took your fire and called it fragility.
But your spark survived."

Another voice.
Another rising.

The Hall vibrated with rising energy—an ache being unsealed.
She walked slowly, intentionally, honoring each voice with her
presence.

Until—she stopped.

One alcove refused her.

She reached for it.
Waited.

Silence.

Then—a voice.
Low. Bitter. Honest:

"I spoke, and they called it venom.
I resisted, and they called me dangerous.
So I made myself small, and they said I was wise."

The walls around her pulsed.

That voice…

It didn't come from history alone.

It came from within.

She clenched her fists, trembling.

You are the part of me I buried.

She stepped closer.

"I see you," she said.
"You are not too much.
You were too real.
I won't leave you here."

The alcove cracked.
Not with collapse—
With release.

And from the fracture stepped a woman—fire in her hands, tears on her face.

She did not disappear.

She walked beside her.

The orb pulsed again—no longer cracked.
Mending.

The Hall shimmered.
The echoes softening.
Not because they had ceased—
But because they had been heard.

She turned toward the path ahead.

Not all the voices had risen.
Not yet.

But some had.

And for now, that was enough.

As she walked forward, something rose in her chest—

The voices weren't just returning.
They were preparing to speak *through her.*

Narrative Reflection

They say memory fades.
But in the Hall, I learned that silence can hold more memory than
sound.
The echoes I heard weren't imaginary.
They were inherited.
Layered in the walls.
Woven into my own breath.
And once I heard them—
the stories, the pain, the resilience—
I couldn't un-hear them.
They live in me now.
Not to haunt me, but to speak through me.
I carry more than my own voice.
And I'm learning not just to echo—
but to answer.

Prophetic Reflection – *Daughter, Arise*

Daughter of Voice,
you who have swallowed your truth to keep the peace—
This is your return.
Your silence was never a flaw.
It was a holding place.
A sacred pause.
But the time for quiet has passed.
Let your voice rise—not in volume, but in resonance.
You are not too loud.
You are aligned.
You carry the song of your ancestors,
the wisdom of the unheard,
the fire of every woman who waited to speak through you.
Now, Daughter—
Speak.

She Is Now Visible – *The Resounder*

She wasn't always sure her voice mattered.
She spent years listening.
Weighing her words.
Choosing safety over truth.
But silence began to ache.
She stopped holding her breath.
Stopped shaping herself to be digestible.
Now when she speaks, it's not to be impressive—
It's to be honest.
And when she tells her story,
people go quiet—
not because they're surprised,
but because they recognize themselves.
Her voice no longer echoes.
It *resounds*.
Because it's no longer waiting.
It's home

CHAPTER 3
THE LABYRINTH OF LETTERS – THE TRUTHKEEPER

There was no entrance.

No threshold. No gate.

One breath, she was in the Hall of Echoes.
The next—here.

The stone beneath her feet was different now.
Engraved with thousands of letters.
Some bold and burning.
Others so faint they flickered like forgotten stars.

The air smelled of burnt parchment, old ink, and ancient breath.

She looked around.

A maze stretched before her—
But not of walls.

Of words.

Scrolls curled around archways.
Broken columns leaned against tablets.
Doorways framed with books that bled language down their spines.

Every direction contradicted the last.
One corridor praised her as a guide.
Another warned her away.
A third simply said:

"Erase her."

This was not a place built to welcome her.

It was built to confuse her.
To rewrite her.

Still—she stepped forward.

The ground shifted beneath her, the letters rearranging with each step.
Some kissed her ankles with warmth.
Others lashed like invisible thorns.
A few tried to cling to her skin, branding her with titles not her own:

"Wife."
"Helper."
"Unnamed woman in the background."
"Daughter of shame."

She stopped.
Breathed.

Her chest tightened—not from fear, but from recognition.

How many times had her identity been written for her?

She pressed her hand to the wall.

"Where is the truth?" she asked.

The labyrinth didn't offer clarity.

It offered a door.

Narrow. Worn. Carved in a language her mind didn't know—
But her spirit did.

She pushed it open.

Inside: a circular room. Small. Still. Sacred.

At its center floated a book.
Bound in leather worn to silver, its pages shimmering—
Alive with breath.

She opened it.

Each page revealed a woman's name, followed by a slash.
Then another name.
Then another.

All of them hers.
All of them rewritten.

She was priest, but they called her pagan.
She was judge, but they called her disobedient.
She was writer, but they called her muse.

Her hands trembled.
Her throat burned.

This wasn't just a maze.

It was a monument to misremembering.

But also—a map.

She returned to the corridors.
This time, she didn't dodge the fragments.

She gathered them.

Torn parchment. Burned corners. Folded truths tucked in cracks.
She carried them like bones.
Like inheritance.

In a hidden alcove, she began to rewrite.

Not with ink.

With presence.

She didn't correct every lie.
She didn't need to.

She named the truth.

One scroll at a time, she whispered:

"She existed."
"She spoke."
"She mattered."

And the labyrinth shifted.

The letters under her feet settled.
No longer hostile.
Aligned.

The corridors straightened.
Doorways opened.

Light poured in—soft. Golden.
Warm as breath.

And then—they stepped forward.

Women.

Some held pens.
Some held charred scraps.
Some held only their names—
Trembling, but whole.

They weren't ghosts.
Not memories.

Witnesses.

One stepped close and asked:

"Will you finish what we began?"

She didn't answer with words.

She nodded.

And walked forward.

The words that once wounded now made way for her.

Not because they had changed—
But because she had claimed the right to write her way through.

Narrative Reflection - After the Labyrinth

I once believed that what was written must be true.
That printed words meant permanence.
But in the Labyrinth, I learned that even truth can be rewritten—
and lies can be codified as legacy.
I saw how names were altered, how stories were stripped,
how identity was folded into footnotes.
But I also saw the fragments—the sacred scraps that survived the fire.
And I understood:
I don't have to recover every erased word.
I just have to remember what they tried to make me forget.
I don't need approval to speak.
I only need breath.

Prophetic Reflection – *Daughter, Arise*

Daughter of Ink and Memory,
you who have been redacted by systems,
rewritten by silence,
reduced to fragments—
This is your reclamation.
You are not too complex.
You are not too inconvenient.
You are the original manuscript.
The one they tried to rename,
but could never unwrite.
Take the pen.
Tell the truth.
Say her name—yours.
Restore the record with your voice.
The pages are not empty.
They are waiting.

She Is Now Visible – *The Truthkeeper*

She was never loud.
But she remembered everything.
The glance that dismissed her.
The meeting where her ideas were renamed.
The story that didn't include her name.
She tried, for a while, to let it go.
To stay silent. To keep peace.
But peace that demands forgetting isn't peace.
It's erasure.
Now she speaks with clarity.
Not to prove a point—
But to pull truth out of the margins.
She doesn't yell.
She doesn't waver.
She just says what's real.
And the room shifts—

Because when she speaks,
What was forgotten gets remembered.

.

CHAPTER 4: THE MIRROR PLAINS - THE MIRRORWALKER

There was no sound when she entered.

Only light—silver and still—stretched endlessly in all directions.

No walls.
No sky.
No horizon.

Only the mirrored ground beneath her feet—
And her own reflection, staring back.

She took a step.

Her reflection didn't move.

She froze.

Another step.

This time, the reflection moved—
But not in sync.
It smiled when she didn't. Tilted its head the wrong way. Blinked too slowly.

Something was wrong.

The ground rippled. The air shimmered.

And then—from beneath the mirrored surface—other versions of her began to rise.
Like memories pulled from deep water.

One was younger—afraid, shoulders hunched, eyes darting.
Another was polished—smiling with empty grace, voice rehearsed to please.

A third stood tall in pride, wrapped in certainty—but her eyes flickered with exhaustion.

Then came the angriest one.

Not screaming.
Seething.

She stepped closer than the others, her voice a low flame:

"You abandoned me when they said I was too much."
"You left me behind when softness got you safety."
"You called me dangerous—because I was honest."

The Woman of Vision staggered backward.

The mirrors responded.

From the ground, more reflections rose.
Not only of who she had been—
But of who others had said she was:

"Too sensitive."
"Too complicated."
"Too loud."
"Too quiet."
"Not enough."
"Too much."

She was surrounded.

Some mirrors mocked.
Some pleaded.
Some wept.

She covered her ears.
But the noise came from within.

Who am I beneath all this?

Then—she saw her.

One reflection, far from the others.
Still. Unmoving. Watching.

She walked toward it.

This one didn't flinch.
Didn't distort.
Didn't pretend.

No costume.
No contortion.
No performance.

Just her.

Whole. Weathered. Awake.

In its eyes—clarity.

She stepped closer.

The reflection opened its mouth and whispered:

"Come back to me."

She fell to her knees.
Tears welled—not from fear.

From relief.

I remember you.

She reached out and placed her hand on the glass.

It was warm.

The mirrors cracked—not from violence, but from release.

The false versions dissolved.
The echoes dimmed.
Only the true self remained, pulsing beneath her hand like a
heartbeat.

She stood.
Straight. Still trembling—but sure.

A path of reflected light unfurled beneath her feet.
Not toward escape—
Toward embodiment.

She no longer feared being seen.

She feared forgetting herself again.

As she walked forward, a final whisper rose behind her—

"When you return to yourself, the world learns how to see."

Narrative Reflection: *The Mirror Plains – I Am*

In the Mirror Plains, I didn't face my past.
I faced my reflection—
and all the versions of myself I had created to survive.
The polite one. The palatable one. The one they praised.
But also—the one I had abandoned.
The true me. The fierce me.
The one who knew who she was before she was named too much.
She didn't blame me.
She waited for me.
And when I met her eyes, I remembered:
I'm not a reflection of their comfort.
I am the revelation they never saw coming.

Prophetic Reflection – *Daughter, Arise*

Daughter of Reflection,
you who have bent yourself into shapes to belong—
Come back to center.
You don't have to perform to be worthy.
You don't have to shrink to be accepted.
You are not the sum of other people's labels.
You are not a distortion.
You are clarity.
You are not a reflection.
You are the image of truth.
Return to yourself.
She has been waiting.
And she's still whole.

She Is Now Visible – *The Mirrorwalker*

She thought her strength came from blending in.
From adjusting her voice, her edges, her truth.
But the mirror showed her all the pieces—
the ones she polished for approval,
the ones she buried to feel safe.
Now, she stands unmasked.
No performance. No pretending.
Not because she has nothing to hide—
but because she finally remembers who she is.
She walks into every room not trying to be liked—
but willing to be seen.
And when people meet her now,
they don't see someone curated.
They see someone *called.*

Chapter 5: The Broken Tower — The Rebuilder

It stood on the edge of a fractured plain—
Leaning, but upright.
Cracked, but not collapsed.

The Tower.

She saw it before she reached it.

Black stone rising into a sky drained of color.
Its upper tiers broken like snapped bone.
The air around it was scorched, silent, heavy with history.

This was not a ruin.
This was a residue.

She moved toward it slowly.

Each step carried the memory of someone who had tried to speak
truth here—and been silenced.
The ground beneath her vibrated with old tension.
It was not a place of safety.

It was a monument to control.

This tower had not been built to uphold justice.
It had been built to enforce silence.

She passed statues long shattered—
Each one headless.
Each one male in form.
None bearing the face of a woman.

The doors loomed tall and rusted.

They opened before she touched them.

Not as a welcome.
As a warning.

Inside, the Tower was vast and hollow.
The echoes clung like webs.

At the center stood a massive stone ledger—
Cracked down the middle.

On one side: names etched deep and glowing, protected by history.
On the other: blank.

Erased.
Forgotten.
Omitted.

She moved toward it.
But the air thickened.
Not with dust—with resistance.

And then—they appeared.

Three figures cloaked in smoke-colored robes.

Their faces hidden behind cracked ivory masks.
Their robes stitched with script.

The **Preservers**.

Not guardians of truth—
Guardians of the system that decided what truth was allowed.

They circled her like shadows.

One spoke, voice sharp as stone:

"You are disturbing the balance."

Another:

"These omissions were necessary."

The third stepped closer:

"Do not open what was sealed."

She said nothing.

She had heard these voices before.

In meetings.
In churches.
In classrooms.

They always sounded reasonable.
Restrained.

They called it history.
But it was hierarchy.

She moved forward.
The Preservers reached toward her—
Chains of red script unraveling from their sleeves.

Words used as weapons.
Doctrines twisted into shackles.
Policies draped in piety.

They tried to bind her hands.
To gag her with protocols.

But she had seen too much.

She had heard too many names.

She tore through the first chain with one word:

"Unsealed."

The second unraveled when she whispered:

"Undesigned."

The third—thick, knotted with fear—melted when she said:

"Unowned."

She placed her hands on the ledger.

And she spoke:

"They were here.
They built.
They led.
They wept.
They endured.
They matter."

The blank side of the ledger began to glow.
Not softly—
But in flame.

The Tower shook.

Stone cracked.
Scrolls burst from the walls.
The Preservers recoiled—
Not in fury.

In exposure.

Their masks cracked.

And beneath—eyes.
Not monstrous.
Human.

But hollowed by the fear of what truth would dismantle.

She didn't shout.

She didn't tear the Tower down in rage.

She stood tall—
Steady.
Still.

She wasn't there to destroy.
She was there to build what should have stood all along.

As she turned to leave, the flames behind her settled into a slow glow.

The Tower didn't fall.

But it would never stand the same again.

And neither would she.

Narrative Reflection: *The Broken Tower – I Stand*

They called it history.
But it was a monument to omission.
The Tower had not fallen—
but it had cracked.
And I realized I didn't come to bring it down.
I came to remember who it had excluded.
And to build what should have been standing in the first place.
It wasn't enough to name the imbalance.
I had to refuse to carry it forward.
Because sometimes standing is the most prophetic thing a woman
can do.

Prophetic Reflection – *Daughter, Arise*

Daughter of Justice,
you who have been asked to be quiet
in the name of "honor,"
in the name of "peace,"
in the name of "order"—
This is your rising.
You were not made to uphold broken blueprints.
You were made to build holy ground.
With truth as your stone.
With memory as your mortar.
You are not here to rage.
You are here to reveal.
And when you stand—
systems tremble.

She Is Now Visible – *The Rebuilder*

She noticed what was missing.
Not just in the stories,
but in the structures.
She heard the silence behind the scrolls,
and it made her ache.
At first, she thought she had to fix it all.
Now, she knows—
she just needs to lay one true stone at a time.
She is not the loudest voice.
But she is the one who doesn't flinch.
She names what needs naming.
She makes space where space was stolen.
And when she builds—
it is not for recognition.
It is for the women who will one day walk through the door she
made.

CHAPTER 6
THE MARKETPLACE OF SHADOWS – THE RESTORER

She smelled it before she saw it.

Smoke.
Metal.
Spice.
Dust.

The air was thick—sweet and strange—like incense burned too long.
It curled around her throat and clung to her ribs.

Before her stretched a vast space:
Tents and tables. Platforms and stages.
A thousand colors, all muted beneath a canopy of shadow.

And people.

Moving like ghosts.

Some silent.
Some selling.
Some being spent.

This was no ordinary market.

It was a **marketplace of offerings**.

But not offerings of goods.

Offerings of self.

She stepped cautiously between the first row of stalls.

A woman stood behind a table, palms outstretched.

"Empathy," she said. Her voice was dull. "I'll carry your burden for free."

Across from her, another woman held silence like a silver tray.

"Peacekeeping," she whispered. "Take what you need. I'll take nothing in return."

Farther down, a third woman smiled through tears.

"Understanding," she said. "Use it. I won't need it where I'm going."

The Woman of Vision stopped.

These women weren't trading.

They were being used.

Drained.
Repackaged.
Spent.

Some stalls bore signs etched in rust:

"Unpaid Counsel"
"Unacknowledged Leadership"
"Invisible Intercession"
"Care Without Credit"

She passed a platform where a woman stood posed like a statue.
Her spine stiff, her hands folded.

The sign below read:

"Strength (as long as it's quiet)"

Another table held piles of journals.
Each one opened to titles:

"What I Never Said"
"What I Gave Away"
"What They Never Thanked Me For"

She reached for one.

But a hand stopped her. Gently.

A woman stood across the table.
Face worn.
Eyes kind.
Hands trembling under the weight of everything she'd carried for everyone else.

"You don't have to carry it anymore," the Woman of Vision said softly.

The woman didn't respond.

She just began to cry.

Not from grief.

From recognition.

Deeper into the market she walked, her chest tightening.

At the center stood a pillar.

Atop it: a crooked scale.
Rust-eaten. Unbalanced.

On one side: a list of what women had given.
On the other: a list of how they had been remembered.

One side overflowed.

The other was nearly blank.

She stepped forward and placed her hand at the base of the scale.

"This is not balance," she whispered.
"This is extraction."

The ground shifted.

And one by one, the stalls began to vanish.

Not with fire.
Not with force.

They disappeared.

Because they were never meant to last.

As she retraced her steps, she saw them—

The women no longer behind their offerings.

They stood beside them.

Not waiting to be spent.

Waiting to be seen.

She didn't come to buy.
She didn't come to take.

She came to return worth to what was never meant to be sold.

She turned to leave the market.

And as she did, the shadows lifted.

Not fully.

But enough for light to find their faces again.

Narrative Reflection:
The Marketplace of Shadows – I Belong

This wasn't a market of goods.
It was a market of selves.
I watched as women traded empathy for survival,
peacekeeping for safety,
identity for access.
And I realized—I had done it too.
I had given without rest.
Loved without boundaries.
Served without being seen.
But I don't want to be consumed anymore.
I want to be known.
Not for what I offer—
But for who I am.

Prophetic Reflection – *Daughter, Arise*

Daughter of Worth,
you who have given yourself away in fragments—
This is your homecoming.
You don't need to prove your heart.
You don't need to apologize for your fullness.
You don't need to earn belonging with exhaustion.
You were never created to be a resource.
You were created to be a revelation.
The sacred cannot be bartered.
And neither can you.
Rise.
And rest.
You are already enough.

She Is Now Visible – *The Restorer*

She was the dependable one.
The peacemaker. The emotional backbone.
She gave until there was nothing left.
And still…
they asked for more.
But one day, she stopped.
Not out of bitterness—
out of wisdom.
She began to ask:
What would it look like to give from overflow, not depletion?
Now, she gives differently.
Not to be needed.
But because she is whole.
She still shows up.
But she doesn't disappear when she does.
She belongs.
Not because she's useful—
But because she's worthy.

Daughter, Arise – A Prophetic Reflection

Daughter of Worth,

You who have given what was sacred
just to be allowed to stay in the room—

This is your return.

You were not born to be palatable.
You were not made to be manageable.

You were never meant to barter your brilliance
or offer your empathy as currency.

Your peacekeeping is not proof of your worth.
Your silence is not holiness.

Heaven saw every labor you gave in secret.

And Heaven calls you whole.

You don't need to earn your place anymore.

You *are* the place.

Stand, Daughter.

Empty your hands of what they demanded.
And lift them—open, holy, whole.

She Is Visible – The Restorer

She was always the helper.
The one they called strong.
The one who stayed.

They praised her for what she gave—
But they never asked what it cost her.

She gave until it ached.
Until there was nothing left for herself.

But one day, she asked the question:

"What would happen if I stopped giving everything away?"

At first—guilt.
Then—grief.
Then… freedom.

Now, she gives from a place of wholeness.
Not depletion.
Not desperation.

She no longer performs selflessness to prove she's worthy.

She knows she already is.

And when they ask what changed?

She says,

"I remembered I was not a product. I was a presence."

Chapter 7
The Silent Sanctuary – The Flamebearer

The path narrowed.

Not with threat.
But with invitation.

No signs marked the way.
No voices called her forward.
Only the steady rhythm in her chest, guiding her into the hush.

The air shifted.
The wind stilled.

Before her rose a structure—small, circular, low to the earth.
Unadorned.
Stone-walled.
Timeless.

The **Sanctuary**.

Its doorway stood open.
No lock. No inscription. No test.

Just presence.

She stepped inside.

Silence met her—not absence, but fullness.
Not the quiet of nothingness,
But the sacred hush of everything waiting.

There was no altar.
No oracle.
No instruction.

Only a fire.

Small.
Centered.
Encircled by ash.

Its embers pulsed faintly—like a breath still warm in the world.

She knelt beside it.

Not to reignite.
To listen.

The floor was covered in thread—golden, nearly invisible—woven
from edge to edge.
Stories sewn into stillness.
Names stitched into silence.

She placed her hand above the embers.

They flared once.
Not with heat.
With memory.

And she remembered—

Every name.
Every voice.
Every rising and revelation.

The Citadel. The Hall. The Labyrinth. The Mirror. The Tower. The
Marketplace.

Each chamber had offered her a flame.
Each one had kindled something within.

But here, in the Sanctuary,
She did not carry them.

She had become them.

From the shadows, they stepped forward—

Not as ghosts.
Not as guides.
But as sisters.

The Queen.
The Builder.
The Resounder.
The Truthkeeper.
The Mirrorwalker.
The Rebuilder.
The Restorer.

They did not speak.

They did not need to.

They surrounded her.
Not to shield.
But to witness.

Their presence was a covenant.

She stood slowly.
Tears on her face.
Not of sorrow.

Of knowing.

This Sanctuary was never meant to contain.

It was built to send.

She turned toward the open doorway.

No longer waiting to be called.
Already commissioned.

As she stepped through the threshold, the embers behind her stirred once more.
And a whisper rose—not from the fire.

From within:

"You are the sanctuary now."

Narrator's Reflection – *After the Sanctuary*

I thought the end would feel like closure.
But it doesn't.
It feels like a beginning.

I don't know exactly where this will lead.
But I know this:

I can never return to the version of myself
who believed her fire had to stay hidden.
I've seen too much.
Heard too much.
Become too much light to go dim again.

And I finally believe—
I was never waiting for a sign.
I am the sign.

Daughter, Arise – *A Prophetic Reflection*

Daughter of Flame,
you who have walked through silence and memory,
you who have risen through forgetting and fire—

This is your awakening.

You don't need another confirmation.
You don't need permission.
You don't need a new invitation.

You are already lit.
You have touched the truth.
You have held the weight of women before you.
You have seen yourself without shame.

And now—
you are not waiting to be sent.
You are the sending.

This Sanctuary is not a hiding place.
It is a launching ground.

Go visible.
Go vital.
Go lit.

You are the Flamebearer.

She Is Now Visible – *The Flamebearer*

She didn't ask to lead.
She didn't chase visibility.
She simply stopped hiding.

Her light was never loud.
Never flashy.
But it was faithful.
Persistent.
Present.
Holy.

At first, they overlooked her.
Then they underestimated her.

But now—
they see it.

Because the warmth became fire.
And the fire became voice.
And the voice became truth.

She no longer waits to be invited in.
She walks in carrying light.

And when she speaks?
The atmosphere shifts.

Because when she enters a room—
the room remembers who it is.

You are the fire now.
Go.

Epilogue – The Gate of Return

I don't remember standing up.
I only remember the weight in my hands—
the warmth of the stone still pulsing, not with heat, but with memory.

The silence around me had changed.
It wasn't empty.
It was full.

The others at the site kept brushing bones, sorting pottery—
still cataloging history like it was over.
But I…
I had been claimed by something alive.

That night, I sat in my tent, journal open, pen in hand.
The pages weren't blank because I had no words.
They were blank because I finally understood:

Some truths don't begin on the page.
They begin in the becoming.

And so I wrote the first name.
Not hers.
Mine.

The Gate of Return is still open.
It doesn't need to be closed.

Because it no longer lives in stone.
It lives in me.

Afterword: You Are the Fire

A Final Blessing and Invitation

You have walked the mist.
Listened in the silence.
Spoken through the ache.
Remembered what was erased.
Reflected what was true.
Stood in what was broken.
Restored what was devalued.
And carried the fire home.

This is not the end.
It is your turning point.

You are not leaving this book as the woman who entered it.
Because this wasn't just a story.
It was a mirror.
It was a mantle.
It was a message—
from the women before you
to the woman you're becoming.

You are not invisible anymore.

You are the Revealer.
The Resounder.
The Truthkeeper.
The Mirrorwalker.
The Rebuilder.
The Restorer.
The Flamebearer.

You are the sign.
You are the sanctuary.
You are the scroll.

You are the voice that no longer echoes—
because it now leads.

So take this with you:

- When the fog returns, remember: You are meant to see.
- When your voice trembles, remember: You are meant to speak.
- When you feel rewritten, remember: You were the original.
- When you feel unseen, remember: You were never invisible to God.

You don't need more confirmation.
You don't need another permission slip.
You are already lit.

You are not waiting to be sent.
You **are** the sending.
And the Gate of Return?
It was never just a place.
It was a passage—
and you've walked through it.

So go.
Visible.
Vital.
Whole.
Holy.
Flame in your bones.
Name in your mouth.
Fire in your steps.

You are the fire now.

Go.

Final Whisper Before Part Two

Daughter,
You have walked through silence, fire, memory, and return.

You have seen.
You have heard.
You have remembered.

And now?

You must rise.

You don't rise alone.
You rise with every name you've ever carried.
Every truth you've ever reclaimed.
Every flame you've been brave enough to hold.

The gate is open.
The world is waiting.

Step through—
visible.

Part Two: The Visibility Companion
A 7-Chapter Journey of Reflection, Revelation & Rising

Introduction

You've walked the story. Now you are part of it.

The *Visibility Companion* is your sacred space for reflection, remembering, and becoming.
Each chapter of *The Visible Woman* is more than narrative—
It is a mirror.
A map.
A mantle.

This companion was created to help you:

- Process what stirred in you as you read
- Listen to the silences in your own life
- Speak back the truths you've buried
- Claim your voice and walk in visibility—without apology

Each section includes:

- A poetic summary of the chapter's truth
- Reflective questions
- A "Release & Remember" prompt for journaling
- A personal *Visibility Declaration*
- A scripture-based daily devotional for anchoring your rise in Spirit and truth

There is no wrong way to move through this.

Write. Pause. Return.

You are not too late.
You are not too much.
You are exactly where you're meant to rise.

Chapter 1 – The Shrouded Citadel: I See

Chapter Summary
In the fog, the forgetting began.
But beneath the silence was memory, waiting to be re-seen.
The Citadel wasn't just a place.
It was a veil—and now, it's lifting.

Sacred Questions

- Where have I felt hidden, forgotten, or erased?
- What part of me do I sense is waking up again?
- Who have I seen in history or my lineage that was never named?
- What do I see now that I didn't allow myself to before?

Release & Remember
Prompt: *"These are the names I see…"* *(Write freely)*

Visibility Declaration
I see what others overlooked.
I honor what was buried.
I walk with the women who walked before me.
I am the Revealer.

Devotional
Scripture: Genesis 16:13
"You are the God who sees me."

Reflection: The fog was never final. Your sight is sacred.

Prayer:
God of the Hidden and Holy, help me see what You have never stopped seeing. Amen.

Chapter 2 – The Hall of Echoes: I Hear

Chapter Summary
The silence wasn't empty.
It was heavy with voices waiting to rise.
To hear is to honor. And now, you become the keeper of echoes.

Sacred Questions

- What truths have I quieted to keep the peace?
- Whose voice am I being asked to honor or amplify?
- Where do I feel called to listen more deeply—within or around me?

Release & Remember
Prompt: *"These are the voices I will no longer ignore…"*

Visibility Declaration
I was not born to echo fear.
I was born to resound with truth.
I carry the voices of those who were silenced.
I am the Resounder.

Devotional
Scripture: 1 Samuel 3:10
"Speak, Lord, for your servant is listening."

Reflection: Listening is sacred work. You're not just hearing—you're witnessing.

Prayer:
God of memory and mercy,
make me a keeper of what was silenced. Amen.

Chapter 3
The Labyrinth of Letters: I Remember

Chapter Summary
Truth had been rewritten. But you were born to restore what was lost.
You are not a revision. You are the voice they tried to erase.

Sacred Questions

- What stories of mine have been edited or suppressed?
- Where have I accepted someone else's version of my truth?
- What am I ready to reclaim with authority?

Release & Remember
Prompt: *"This is the truth I am writing back into the world..."*

Visibility Declaration
I do not need permission to speak.
I do not need validation to write.
I was not erased—I am restored.
I am the Truthkeeper.

Devotional
Scripture: Habakkuk 2:2
"Write the vision and make it plain..."

Reflection:
Some truths rise as fire. You are the one sent to name them.

Prayer:
God of the Word, let my voice become the restoration. Amen.

Chapter 4 – The Mirror Plains: I Am

Chapter Summary
The mirror did not lie. It simply waited for you to see. What you thought was 'too much' was actually your truth—undistorted.

Sacred Questions

- What parts of myself have I hidden to be accepted?
- Where have I mirrored false reflections to survive?
- Who am I beneath the performance?

Release & Remember
Prompt:
"This is who I am beneath the reflection…"

Visibility Declaration
I am not a reflection of fear.
I am whole. I am home.
I am the Mirrorwalker.

Devotional
Scripture: 1 Corinthians 13:12 — *"Then I shall know fully, even as I am fully known."*
Reflection: Knowing yourself is prophetic work.
Prayer: *God of clarity, let me meet the woman You always knew I was. Amen.*

Chapter 5 – The Broken Tower: I Stand

Chapter Summary
You were not meant to uphold what oppresses.
You are not a destroyer—you are a rebuilder.

Sacred Questions

- What structures have required my silence or complicity?
- Where am I being called to name what's broken?
- What new foundation am I called to lay?

Release & Remember
Prompt:
"Here is what I will no longer protect with my silence…"

Visibility Declaration
I will not uphold what harms.
I will not shrink to fit a lie.
I am the Rebuilder.

Devotional
Scripture: Proverbs 9:1
"Wisdom has built her house…"

Reflection:
Wisdom doesn't preserve injustice. It lays new stones.

Prayer:
God of justice and blueprints, teach me to build with truth.
Amen.

Chapter 6
The Marketplace of Shadows: I Belong

Chapter Summary
You were not made to be spent.
Your worth is not in your sacrifice—it's in your *being*.

Sacred Questions

- What have I been giving away for belonging?
- Where have I allowed my value to be measured by others?
- What does sacred, self-honoring giving look like for me?

Release & Remember
Prompt:
"This is what I take back as mine…"

Visibility Declaration
I do not trade my truth for approval.
I give from wholeness, not exhaustion.
I am the Restorer.

Devotional
Scripture: 1 Corinthians 6:19-20
"You are not your own; you were bought at a price."

Reflection:
You don't belong to the marketplace. You belong to the Divine.

Prayer: *God of sacred worth, remind me I am never for sale. Amen.*

Chapter 7 – The Silent Sanctuary: I Rise

Chapter Summary
This was not an ending. This was a sending.
You don't just carry the fire. You *are* the flame.

Sacred Questions

- What fire is burning in me now?
- How am I being sent—not later, but now?
- What must I release in order to rise?

Release & Remember
Prompt: *"This is the fire I carry forward..."*

Visibility Declaration
I am already chosen.
I walk in light.
I am the Flamebearer.

Devotional
Scripture: Isaiah 60:1
"Arise, shine, for your light has come,
and the glory of the Lord has risen upon you"

Reflection:
You are not waiting to be called. You are walking already.

Prayer: *God of sending and sacred fire, let me carry the light forward. Amen.*

Dr. Andrea Williams

Afterword: You Are the Fire

A Final Blessing and Invitation

You have walked the seven chambers.
You have listened to the voices that were buried.
You have seen what was hidden.
And you have remembered who you are.

You were not called to remain in waiting.
You were not awakened to stay silent.
You were not healed to become invisible again.

You are not simply *someone who read a book*.
You are someone who has crossed a threshold.

The gate is not behind you.
The gate is within you.
And you are walking through it.

So take this with you:

- When the world grows loud again,
  return to silence, and remember what you heard.
- When the fog creeps back in,
  return to the citadel, and remember what you saw.
- When the names feel lost,
  return to the mirror, and say your own with boldness.

You are not returning to life as usual.
You are returning *as one who has seen*.

One who carries fire.

And now…

You are the sanctuary.
You are the scroll.
You are the sign.
You are the voice that no longer echoes—
because it now leads.

Go visible.
Go boldly.
Go lit.

The time is not coming.
The time is now.

***

Want more space to rise?

If this companion stirred something deeper in you,
If you're ready for pages to write, space to process,
And tools to walk this journey further...

The **Expanded Visibility Workbook** includes:

- Full journaling spreads
- Group study discussion prompts
- Weekly integration practices
- Visibility rituals and declarations
- A 30-day Visibility Prayer Journey

✦ Available soon wherever books are sold.
Or visit me on my Substack (@AndreaWilliamsGlobal) to subscribe
and join the *Visible Women Rising* community.

You've remembered.

Now... you *become*.

Dr. Andrea Williams

ABOUT THE AUTHOR

Bishop Dr. Andrea Williams is the Senior Minister of Ebenezer International Ministries, located in Fishers, Indiana.
She is a proud mother of three sons and a grandmother of five wonderful grandchildren.

Bishop Andrea is an ordained Apostle and Prophet and was consecrated to the office of the Bishopric in 2018. As an avid encourager of education, both spiritually and naturally, Bishop Andrea holds a BA in religious studies, MA & Th.D. in Theology, and attained her D.Min in 2025. Bishop Dr. Andrea Williams is a seasoned prophet with a relevant word from the Lord and travels extensively throughout America and other nations equipping men and women for the purpose for which they were created.

Bishop Andrea has been gifted with a versatile voice to impact the Body of Christ as well as community, the public-school system, millennials and women throughout the world.

Her voice is heard in several formats as a prolific writer, speaker, equipper, and activist.
Here are some of Dr. Williams' written works:

- *A Woman's Place Is In…*
- *Thus Saith The Lord*
- *Deborahs Unveiled – Devotional Journal*
- *In Search of Hope*
- *The Place Called There*
- School of the Prophet Training Manuals:
  * *School of The Prophet: Basic Training*
  * *SOP: The Next Level*

For booking or scheduling Dr. Andrea Williams for speaking engagements or training, please contact:
BishopAndreaWilliams@gmail.com
(317) 813-9840

AndreaWilliamsMinistries.com

Made in the USA
Las Vegas, NV
06 June 2025

bf14a806-da34-4ba4-bdc4-e19942231ec4R01